UP
CLOSE

BUTTERFLIES
A CLOSE-UP PHOTOGRAPHIC LOOK INSIDE YOUR WORLD

Written by Heidi Fiedler

This library edition published in 2017 by Walter Foster Jr.,
an imprint of The Quarto Group
6 Orchard Road, Suite 100
Lake Forest, CA 92630

Project Editor: Heidi Fiedler
Written by Heidi Fiedler
Photographs on pages 3 (top), 7 (center and bottom), 8, 10, 14,
26-27, and 28 by Igor Siwanowicz.
All other images © Shutterstock.

Distributed in the United States and Canada by
Lerner Publisher Services
241 First Avenue North
Minneapolis, MN 55401 U.S.A.
www.lernerbooks.com

First Library Edition

Library of Congress Cataloging-in-Publication Data

Names: Fiedler, Heidi, author.
Title: Butterflies : a close-up photographic look inside your world / written
   by Heidi Fiedler.
Description: First library edition. | Lake Forest, CA : Walter Foster
   Publishing, an imprint of The Quarto Group, 2017. | Audience: Ages 8+. |
   Includes bibliographical references and index.
Identifiers: LCCN 2017011658 | ISBN 9781942875376 (hardcover : alk. paper)
Subjects: LCSH: Butterflies--Juvenile literature. | Caterpillars--Juvenile
   literature. | Cocoons--Juvenile literature. | Photography,
   Close-up--Juvenile literature.
Classification: LCC QL544.2 .F54 2017 | DDC 595.78/9--dc23
LC record available at https://lccn.loc.gov/2017011658

Printed in USA
9 8 7 6 5 4 3 2 1

MIX
Paper from
responsible sources
FSC® C008080

Are You Ready for Your Close-up?

Can you feel your brain tickling? That's the magic of looking at something way UP CLOSE. It transforms the ordinary into something new and strange, and inspires everyone from hi-tech shutterbugs and supersmart scientists to look again. So let's turn the ZOOM up to eleven and discover a whole new way of seeing the world.

Tussock caterpillar

How Eye See the World

"Whatcha lookin' at?" That's the question people have been asking each other for thousands of years. The first humans observed interesting—and important—things like woolly mammoths, lightning, and each other. Early artists moved on to painting and drawing what they saw. Finally, in 1862, photography allowed people to capture what they saw in new and amazing ways.

Today, photographs are everywhere. Cereal boxes, bulletin boards, and T-shirts are all home to photos. A simple image search online can produce cootchie-cootchie-coo images of bright-eyed babies or stark, white, snowy landscapes. Photographers capture everything from moments of joy and pain to the wonders that exist in the cracks and hidden layers of our busy world. They focus their attention on a huge range of subjects, and the images they produce reveal how everyone sees the world in their own unique way.

The History of Photography

| Black-and-White Photography | **1826** Nicéphore Niépce creates the first photograph. It takes 8 hours. | **1859** Photography goes panoramic. | **1839** Daguerreotypes capture rough images on pieces of metal. | **1877** Eadweard Muybridge invents a way to shoot objects—such as horses—in motion. |

Color Photography

1888
Kodak™ produces the first mass-produced camera.

1912
The 35mm camera takes center stage.

1930
Flash bulbs help photographers capture images in low light.

1935
New techniques make color photography shine.

1939
An electron microscope reveals what a virus looks like.

1946
Zoomar produces the zoom lens.

Digital Photography

1976
Canon® produces the first camera with a microprocessor.

"Photography...has little to do with the things you see and everything to do with the way you see them."
—Elliott Erwitt

1992
The first JPEG is produced.

2015
Instagram is home to more than 20 billion images.

Extreme Close-up!

Photography has been helping people express how they see the world for nearly 200 years, and in that time, things have gone way beyond taking a simple shot of a horse or a sunset. Today, photographers are pushing the limits of technology.

Macro photographers use large lenses to get WAY up close to their subjects. They can magnify an object to more than five times its size, using special lenses that reveal patterns and textures that wow viewers.

Black-veined white

Micro photography goes even further. It uses a microscope to reveal details humans could never see before. It can make a butterfly look like a majestic mermaid or a priceless piece of jewelry.

With their vibrant colors and strange shapes, butterflies (and caterpillars) are a favorite subject for photographers. Some shutterbugs are scientists who are thrilled to be able to count exactly how many scales are on a butterfly wing. Other photographers are insect enthusiasts who are obsessed with capturing every hair on a moth's body. Together, their images help us see the natural world in a whole new way.

Peacock swallowtail

Getting the Shot

Photographers choose where and how they want to work based on what type of images they want to produce.

Monarch cocoon

Out in the Field

Macro photographers can take their giant lenses outside to capture insects in their natural environment.

In the Studio

Working inside lets photographers have more control over the lighting, the angle of the camera, and their subject.

Proboscis

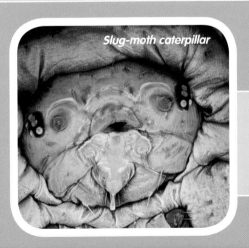
Slug-moth caterpillar

Under the Microscope

A microscope allows photographers to look at their subjects in even more detail.

Hissssss!

Slithering down the branch, this green guy may look like a snake. And that's just the way he likes it. But the spicebush swallowtail is really a peaceful caterpillar that relies on mimicry to scare away predators. It even has a smelly "forked tongue" like a snake.

Instead of looking **smooth** and **sleek** like a **snake**, some **caterpillars** rely on **horns** to look as **tough** as possible.

Scientific Name:
   Papilio troilus
Size: 1.5 to 2 inches
Habitat: North America
Diet: Spicebush and
   other trees

Look Away!

Caterpillars aren't the only ones who think the more eyes the better. Many butterflies, reptiles, birds, and fish use eye spots to look big and bold.

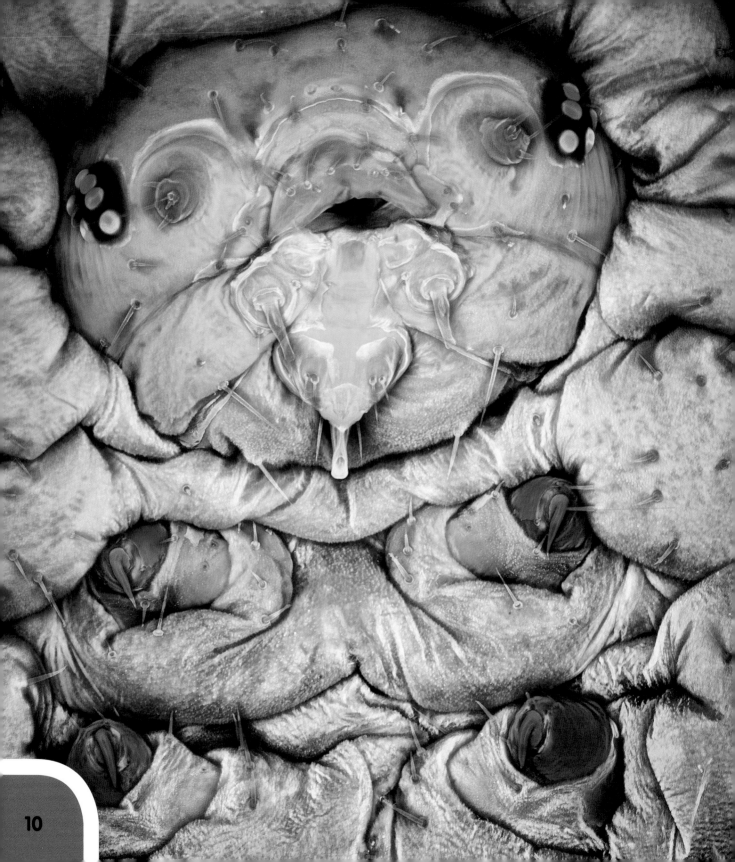

Stuck Between a Camera and a Hard Place

Unlike most caterpillars, which have way too many legs to count, the slug-moth caterpillar has stubby feet that act like suction cups as it travels. They let the caterpillar ripple across leaves at surprisingly high speeds and hang from the underside of the plants it's devouring. Stinging bristles on its back warn anyone who might dare interfere with its meal to stand down.

Yum or Yuck?

Can you guess which of these buggy bites people like eating?

A) ant popcorn
B) beetle sandwiches
C) cricket tacos
D) banana worm bread
E) all of the above

If you answered E, all of the above, you're right!

Scientific Name: Limacodidae
Size: .39 to 1.18 inches
Habitat: Found around the world, especially in the tropics
Diet: The leaves of a variety of plants

In natural **light**, this caterpillar looks like a chubby, neon green leaf. When it **becomes** a **butterfly**, the slug **moth** is **covered** in **fuzzy**, lucky-clover-green **streaks**.

A Golden Time Machine

Every caterpillar is preparing for the day when it will enter its cocoon, turn into a butterfly, and fly away. As a caterpillar grows, it sheds its skin. When the time is right, it shakes off its skin one last time, and a cocoon is revealed. At first it's soft and wet, but soon it hardens. What happens inside is a mystery that scientists are only just beginning to understand.

Cocoons, or **chrysalises**, may look **sleepy**, but if you **watch** carefully, you may **see** them **wiggle** as they **hang** down from the branches.

Cocoons

Cocoons come in as many shapes and sizes as butterflies do. Some look like jellybeans. Others look like snail shells or gold pieces of pasta. And many cocoons change colors as the butterfly grows inside.

Sleeping Beauty

When it's time for a butterfly to leave its cocoon, it pushes its head and legs through the wall. Finally, its wings emerge. At first, they look wet and wrinkled. But as the butterfly pumps blood into the veins, the wings expand to reveal their beautiful colors.

Wigging Out

Sure, the butterfly or moth that emerges from a cocoon can be a dull brown insect. But if you're a giant peacock moth, that won't do. You'll want your antennae to look like the leaves from a tree on a distant planet. Big sunglass-style eyes are totally in. And as for your head? Ooh, la, la. The fluffier the better.

Scientific Name:
  Saturnia pyri
Size: Wingspan is 4 to 6 inches
Habitat: Europe
Diet: Adults don't feed

Polyphemus **moths** use their **long** antennae to **find** a mate and **sense** chemicals in the **air**.

Wild Wings

It's hard to look at a caterpillar and know what kind of moth is going to pop out of the cocoon. The bright green caterpillar might turn into an orange moth, a red moth, or one of the other beauties below.

Cecropia moth

Elephant hawk-moth

Bee hawk-moth

Striped hawk-moth

My, what big eyes you have...

Eyes Up Front!

Eye see you! The peacock butterfly's distinct eyespots and red wings confuse and intimidate predators—they see the eyespots and think the butterfly is one of their enemies.

Tastes like feet!

Butterflies have taste sensors on their feet, which means they can taste their food as soon as they land on it! This handy (or footy!) way of tasting food helps when they lay their eggs— they can taste a leaf to see if their caterpillars can eat it when they hatch.

Scientific Name:
  Aglais io
Size: 2 inches
Habitat: Europe and Asia
Diet: Nectar, sap, and fruit

Butterflies get their **color** from **millions** of **scales** that overlap like roof shingles.

Herald moth

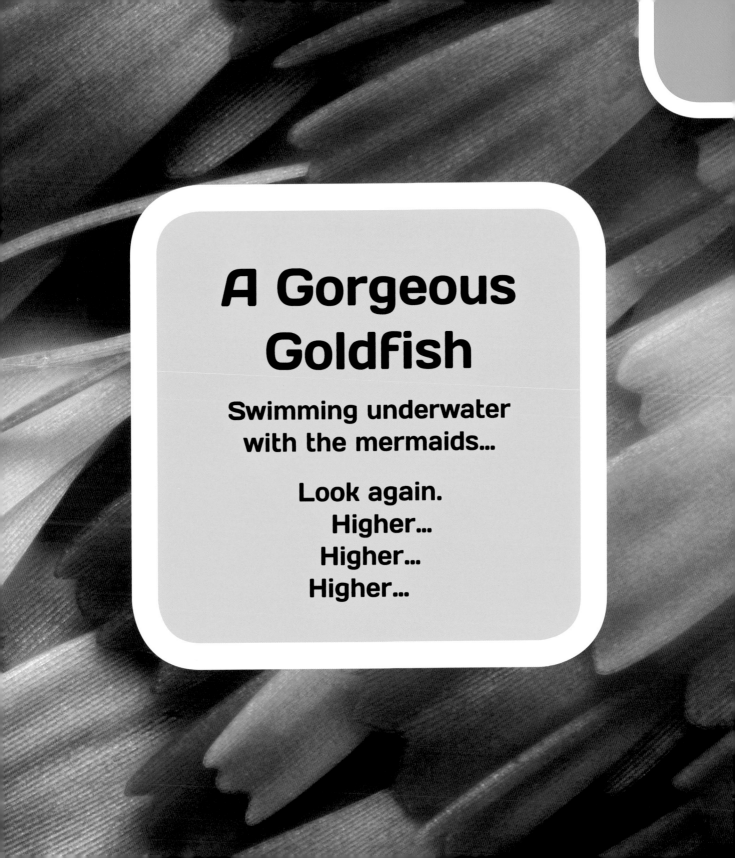

A Gorgeous Goldfish

**Swimming underwater
with the mermaids...**

**Look again.
Higher...
Higher...
Higher...**

It's a Rainbow in the Sky!

Butterflies are the fashionistas of the insect world, showing off their couture colors as they fly through the air. But their bright wings aren't just for show. They help butterflies attract mates, scare away predators, and hide among the flowers.

Green-spotted triangle

Sunset moth

Shiny Like a Lollipop

Hidden Colors

Red admiral

Old world swallowtail

The Stunning Swallowtail

Royal Bloodlines

Blue Morpho

Monarch

A Magnificent Monarch

Fairy Wings

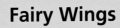

Peacock swallowtail

Spiraling Down
Down...
Down...
Down...

**Do dark stairways ever lead anywhere good?
Depends what you're hungry for.**

Slurp!

If you're an insect, chances are you're hungry for sugar! Some butterflies and moths don't have mouths at all. They do all the eating they will ever do as caterpillars. But those that have mouths usually have a proboscis. It works just like one of those crazy twisty straws you get at the circus. Butterflies and moths unfurl their long tongues to reach the sweet, sweet nectar inside flowers. When they're not sucking up sugar, the proboscis is coiled up inside their mouths.

Moths are **nocturnal**. More than **150,000** species **hit** the **sky** each **night**.

Scientific Name:
Apatura iris
Size: Wingspan can reach up to 3.5 inches
Habitat: Woodlands of Central Europe and Asia

Moths Versus Butterflies

How can you tell the difference between moths and butterflies?

Moths		Butterflies
Feathery or ragged	**Antennae**	Long and club shaped
Hold their wings like a tent over their abdomen	**Wings**	Fold their wings over their backs
Smaller	**Size**	Larger
Often dull and brown	**Color**	Come in a rainbow of colors
Most are nocturnal	**Active**	Fly most often during the day
Builds a silk cocoon	**Metamorphosis**	Makes a hard, smooth chrysalis

Behind the Lens

Now it's your turn! Grab a camera and start shooting whenever you see something that amazes you or makes you curious to learn more. If you want to go macro without spending too much money, snap a macro lens band over a cellphone camera. Whatever camera you use, these tips will help you get started.

The flash lights the subject.

The shutter acts like a camera, opening and closing to let light into the camera for short periods of time.

The lens is the curved piece of glass that light travels through before reaching a sensor or film inside the camera.

A tripod keeps the camera steady.

The size of the opening in the lens is the aperture. It's measured in fractions.

The focal point is the part of the image that's sharp.

The depth of field is the distance between the parts of an object that are in focus. In micro and macro photography, this distance is very small.

Some lenses have a short focal length and produce a wider angle of view. Other lenses have a longer focal length.

Aperture Scale

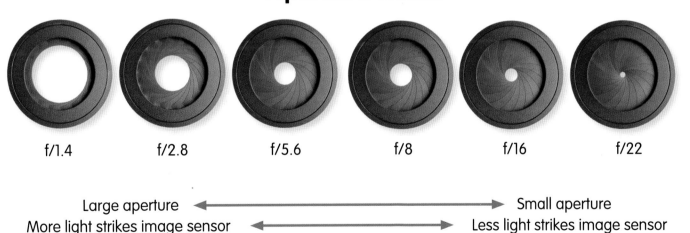

| f/1.4 | f/2.8 | f/5.6 | f/8 | f/16 | f/22 |

Large aperture ⟷ Small aperture
More light strikes image sensor ⟷ Less light strikes image sensor
Shallow Depth of Field (Focus) ⟷ Deep Depth of Field (Focus)

Index

Old world swallowtail